MOSQUITOES

INSECTS IN MY BACKYARD

RYAN JAMES

NorwoodHouse Press

Library of Congress Cataloging-in-Publication Data

Names: James, Ryan.
Title: Mosquitos / Ryan James.
Description: Buffalo, NY : Norwood House Press, 2025. | Series: Insects in my backyard | Includes glossary and index.
Identifiers: ISBN 9781684502530 (pbk.) | ISBN 9781684502547 (library bound) | ISBN 9781684502554 (ebook)
Subjects: LCSH: Mosquitoes--Juvenile literature.
Classification: LCC QL536.J359 2025 | DDC 595.77'2--dc23

Published in 2025 by
Norwood House Press
2544 Clinton Street
Buffalo, NY 14224

Designer: Ocean Books
Editor: Kim Thompson

Photo credits: Cover, p. 1 jiade/Shutterstock.com; p. 5 Kwangmoozaa/Shutterstock.com; p. 7 Naturesports/Shutterstock.com; p. 9 ErickPHOTOPRO/Shutterstock.com; p. 11 InsectWorld/Shutterstock.com; p. 12 Mario Saccomano/Shutterstock.com; p. 13 Centers for Disease Control and Prevention; p. 15 Sahin Tokmak/Shutterstock.com; p. 16 NuayLab/Shutterstock.com; p. 17 Sean McCann; p. 18 MarcinSl1987/Shutterstock.com; p. 19 WindOpHope/Shutterstock.com; p. 21 Tonhom1009/Shutterstock.com

Printed in the United States of America

TABLE OF CONTENTS

WHAT IS A MOSQUITO?

Mosquitoes are flying **insects** that you might find in your backyard. They come out mostly at night. They can bite people and animals.

BODY PARTS

Mosquitoes have three body sections. The head is in front. A mosquito's head is small, but its eyes are large. Long **antennae** help mosquitoes find food and mates.

Female mosquitoes use a long, sharp mouthpart to bite animals and drink their blood.

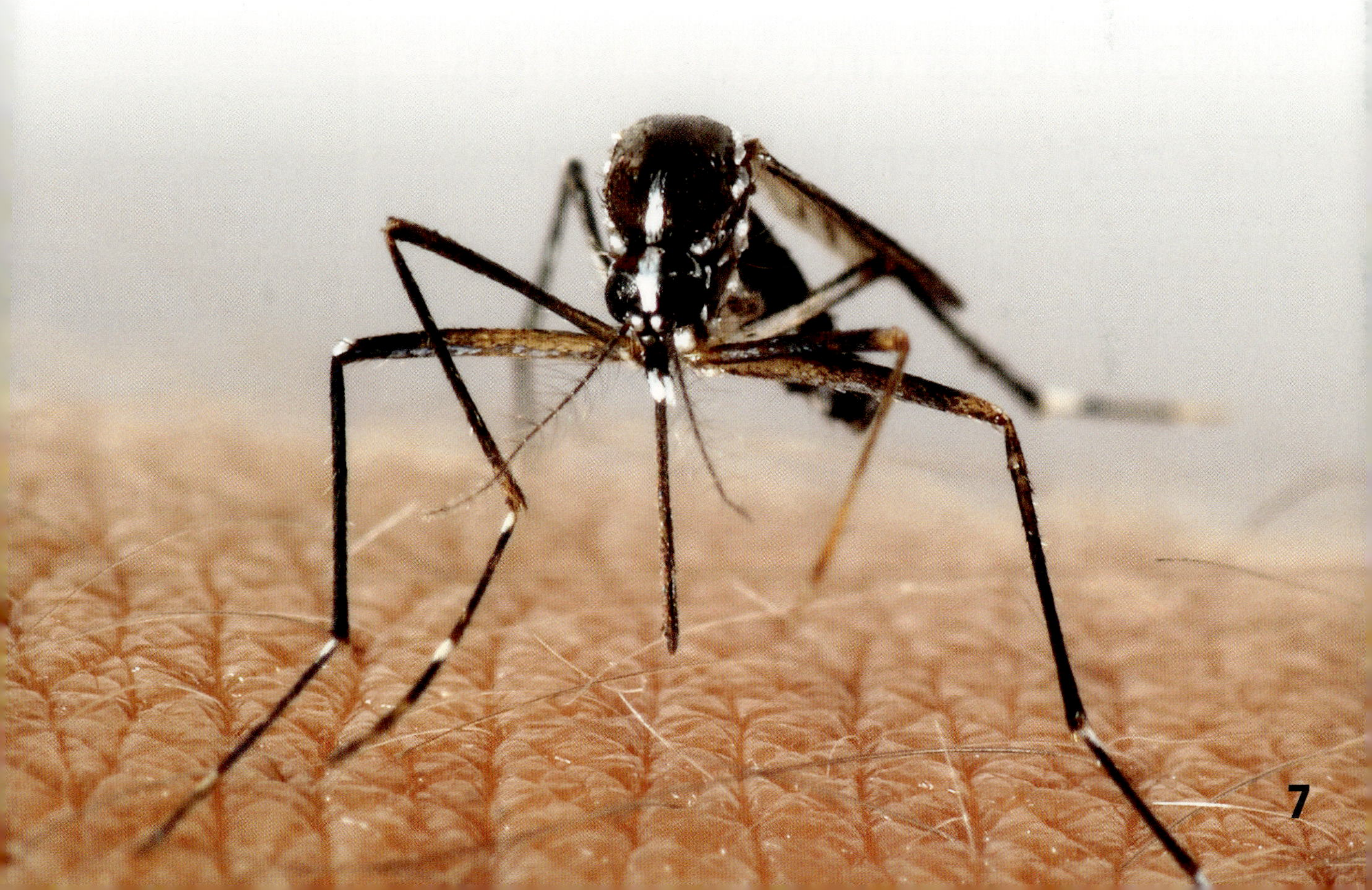

The thorax is the middle of a mosquito's body. It has six long legs and two wings. The abdomen is the back of a mosquito's body. It can swell when mosquitoes eat.

TYPES OF MOSQUITOES

The small Aedes mosquito has black and white stripes on its legs. It is found in the United States and in many **tropical** areas of the world.

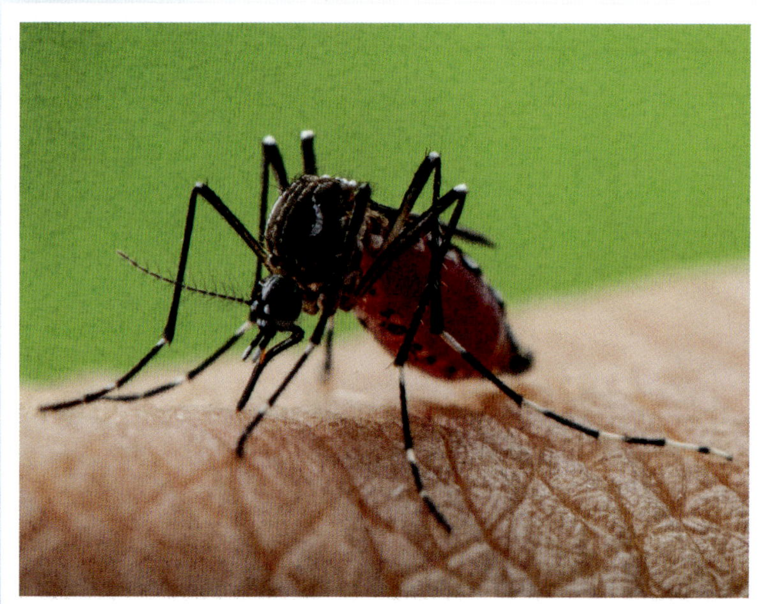

The Asian tiger mosquito has black and white stripes on its body and legs. It is common in Asia, but it is also found in the U.S. and Europe.

The Culex mosquito is light brown. It is common in North America and Asia.

The Anopheles mosquito is brown with spotted wings. It is common in Africa. This mosquito can spread **malaria**.

MOSQUITO BEHAVIOR

Mosquitoes come out mostly at night to find food. They are attracted to body heat and to the **carbon dioxide** that people and animals breathe out.

Female mosquitoes bite to drink blood, which they need to lay eggs. Male mosquitoes feed on **nectar** from flowers.

Mosquitoes lay eggs in standing water. The eggs hatch into **larvae** that live in the water until they become adults.

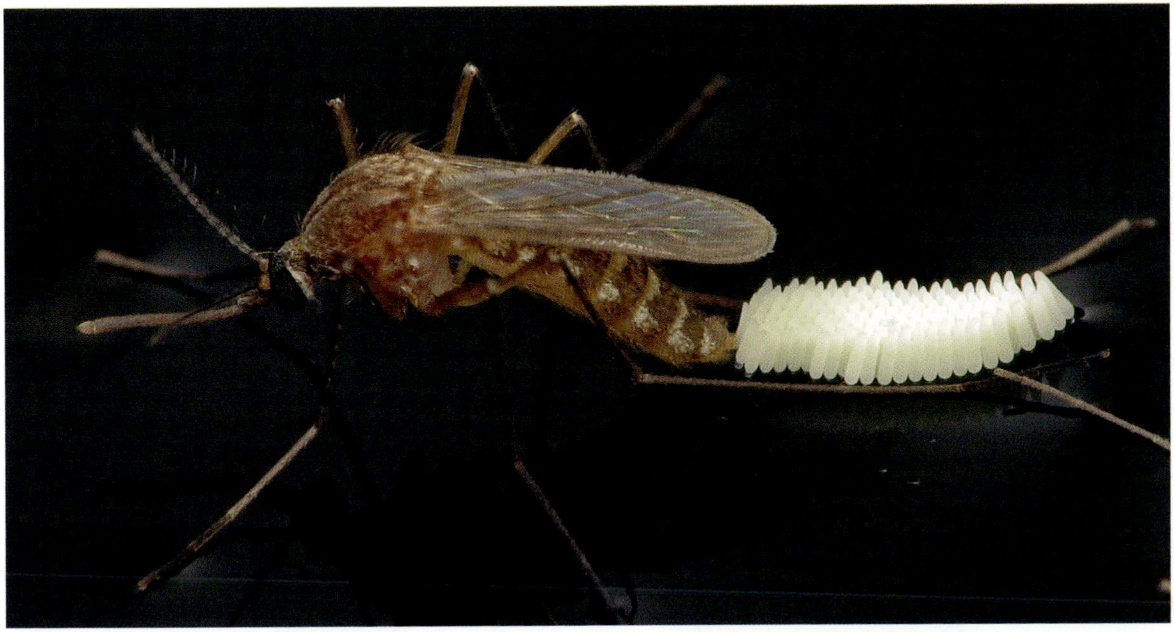

WHY ARE MOSQUITOES IMPORTANT?

Mosquitoes are food for many animals like birds, bats, and fish. They are an important part of the food chain.

Mosquitoes that feed on flowers carry **pollen** from plant to plant. This helps many plants make seeds and fruit.

Scientists study mosquitoes to learn about the diseases they spread. This helps people find ways to prevent and treat malaria, Zika, and other illnesses.

GLOSSARY

antennae (an-TEN-ee): slender, movable, segmented organs on the heads of insects that are used to sense the environment; feelers

carbon dioxide (KAHR-buhn dye-AHK-side): a gas that is a mixture of carbon and oxygen and that has no odor or color; people and animals breathe this gas out while plants take it in

insects (IN-sekts): small animals that have hard outer skeletons instead of backbones and that have three pairs of legs, one or two pairs of wings, and three body sections

larvae (LAHR-vee): insects at a stage of development after they hatch from eggs, when they look like worms

malaria (muh-LAIR-ee-uh): a serious disease that is spread by mosquito bites and that gives people chills, fever, and sweating

nectar (NEK-tur): a sweet liquid produced by flowers

pollen (PAH-luhn): fine yellow powder that is produced in the male parts of flowering plants and that must be spread to female plant parts in order for some plants to reproduce

tropical (TRAH-pi-kuhl): of or having to do with regions of the world that are always hot and rainy

THINKING QUESTIONS

1. Name a mosquito's three body sections.
2. How are an Asian tiger mosquito and a Culex mosquito alike and different?
3. How do mosquitoes grow up?
4. How do mosquitoes help plants?
5. Why are mosquitoes important?

INDEX

ABOUT THE AUTHOR

Ryan James lives in the western part of North Carolina with his rescue dog Bailey. As a child, he would search for creepy crawlies as he hiked through the forest near his house. When he's not on the hiking or biking trail, he is cheering on his favorite baseball and football teams.